D0581957

Chapters of Gold

THE LIFE OF MARY IN MOSAICS

Phil Sayer

Chapters of Gold

THE LIFE OF MARY IN MOSAICS

RACHEL BILLINGTON

PHOTOGRAPHY BY GERED MANKOWITZ

BURNS & OATES
A *Continuum imprint*
LONDON • NEW YORK

First published 2003 by Continuum
The Tower Building, 11 York Road, London SE1 7NX
www.continuumbooks.com

Editorial Director: Joseph Bonner
Art Editor: Julie Bennett
Designer: Paolo Albertazzi

With thanks to Fr Richard Andrew, Elizabeth Benjamin, Fr Timothy Dean, Nicole Runge, Fr Michael Seed sa, Rebecca Thomas and Oremus - The magazine of Westminster Cathedral.

© 2003 Westminster Cathedral
42 Francis Street, London SW1P 1QW
www.westminstercathedral.org.uk

ISBN 0-8601-2350-2
Printed and bound in Slovenia

Dedicated to Elizabeth, Countess of Longford
1906–2002

PLAN OF THE FRIEZE
DEPICTING MARY'S LIFE
Lady Chapel, Westminster Cathedral

1 Betrothal of Joachim and Anne
2 Birth of Mary
3 Presentation of Mary in the Temple
4 Mary's betrothal to Joseph
5 Annunciation by the Angel Gabriel
6 Visitation of Mary to Elizabeth
7 Nativity at Bethlehem
8 Presentation of Jesus in the Temple
9 Flight into Egypt
10 Finding in the Temple
11 Home at Nazareth
12 Marriage Feast at Cana
13 Mary bids farewell to Jesus
14 Way of the Cross
15 Crucifixion
16 News of the resurrection
17 Descent of the Holy Spirit
18 Angel predicts the death of Mary
19 Risen Jesus appears to his Mother
20 Dormition of Mary
21 Saint Luke writing the Gospel

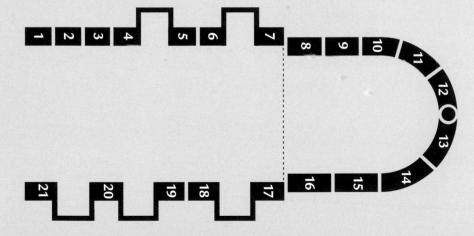

CONTENTS

9 *Foreword* by The Duchess of Kent

10 *Moving our hearts to prayer* Cardinal Cormac Murphy-O'Connor

11 *A life with Christ* Archbishop Rowan Williams

12 *The Life of Mary in mosaics* Lady Rachel Billington

54 *Lady Chapel mosaics - a brief history* Patrick Rogers

56 *A powerful echo of the Orthodox* Gregorios, Archbishop of Thyateira and Great Britain

60 *An aid to devotion* Baroness Kathleen Richardson

62 *A Woman of the House of Imran* Sheikh Dr M A Zaki Badawi

64 *In the House of Life - a personal reflection* Rabbi Lionel Blue

67 *Prayers to the Blessed Virgin Mary* - compiled by Fr Richard Andrew

Foreword

For over 150 years, the Cardinals and Clergy of the Diocese of Westminster have been invaluable mentors and guides to numerous people on their spiritual journeys. And, through this prayerful ministry, seekers of the truth have come closer to understanding something of Mary and her place in the Church.

The Westminster pilgrimage to Lourdes with Cardinal Hume and now with his successor, Cardinal Murphy-O'Connor, has brought countless pilgrims to a place of peace, tranquillity and silence, where people of all faiths can come together, pray and find new hope in their lives.

The comfort of Lourdes is reflected in the Lady Chapel of Westminster Cathedral. High amongst its beautiful mosaics is a scene of Mary appearing to Bernadette at Lourdes. This first part of the Cathedral to be opened for public worship, one hundred years ago, stands complete. To many it stands as a symbol of the glory of God that awaits us.

May those who reflect on these words and photographs of Rachel Billington and Gered Mankowitz find inspiration and peace of mind.

Duchess of Kent

Moving our hearts to prayer

THE Lady Chapel in the Cathedral is a sacred space. It was designed with the intention of moving our hearts to prayer, and our minds to contemplation. The stunning mosaic ceiling recalls the key moments in the life of Mary, and of her son Jesus Christ. It is a fitting tribute to the central role she played in the life of our Lord, and continues to play in the life of the Church.

Somehow the warmth and simplicity of the mosaics seems to invite us to allow ourselves to be moved and inspired by the uniqueness of Mary's relationship to her son. No-one else enjoyed as intimate and loving a relationship with the Saviour of mankind. No-one suffered more on his behalf.

I believe that contemplation of the life of Mary is a valuable way for us to relive the life of Jesus in ways that are imaginative and life-giving. If we enter with imagination into the heart and mind of Mary, we can begin to penetrate that greatest of all mysteries which is the heart and mind of God. And if our response to the Word that we hear, and which is addressed to each of us uniquely, is the same as Mary's - "Let what you have said be done to me" – then we can look forward with hope and confidence that the promises of Christ will be fulfilled in our lives.

If you feel downhearted, as we all do at times, then sit and pray the joyful mysteries and bring to mind the faithfulness and love which Mary cherished in her heart for Jesus her son, and allow yourself to be moved by her example. It can work wonders. If you are able to do that in this Lady Chapel, or any other, so much the better. I hope that this book will draw you deeper into the mystery of the life of God to which Mary's own life points us.

+Cormac Card. Murphy O'Connor

Archbishop of Westminster

A life with Christ

THE mosaics in the Lady Chapel put before us very simply and very beautifully the main thing we need to know about Our Lady: her life is a life with Christ. From the beginning, who she is, is bound up with who Jesus is. We see represented here the legend of her presentation in the Temple as a child - to remind us that her body is always itself the "Holy Place", the sanctuary where God is at home. We see the Gospel stories of her involvement with her Son, her presence at Calvary, her receiving of the resurrection news, her prayer with the Church for the descent of the Holy Spirit and the climax of this life in the Spirit which is her own entry into resurrection glory. When we are alongside her, we are alongside her Son in his suffering and in his glory.

So when we follow Mary's story in these pictures, or when we recite the Rosary, we are putting ourselves with her at her Son's side. And we are - surely - praying that our lives will become more like hers: shaped and marked by her Son at every moment until we enjoy his company for ever in the risen life we are promised; open to the Holy Spirit who will make us all sons and daughters of God, and "bearers" of Christ in the world.

+ Rowan Cantuar:

Archbishop of Canterbury

"Hail Holy
Queen, Mother
of Mercy.
Hail our
Life, our
Sweetness and
our Hope"

HERMANN
CONTRACTUS 1054

Betrothal of Joachim and Anne, Mary's parents

ARY bursts into history with the New Testament's dramatic description of the Annunciation. A young Jewish girl is surprised by an angel who brings to her a message from God. They speak to each other and she accepts the extraordinary future that is offered. It is like a scene on stage, lit brilliantly for a short time, before darkness descends once more. All the recorded events in Mary's life - the Annunciation, the Visitation, the Finding in the Temple, the Marriage Feast of Cana and the others - seem like scenes in a play which dissolve into the darkness of the wings. Mary's birth and upbringing lies hidden in this obscurity. But where there is an absence, tradition, based often on the later writings of the Apocrypha, provides continuity. The Lady Chapel draws on such sources. Tradition has given her parents, St Joachim and St Anne their own saint's day on 21 November. Posterity assumed that Mary, the mother of Jesus, the mother of God, must have had very special parents. They, after all, are the grandparents of Jesus. St Anne is often pictured with Mary and Mary's child, the founding mother of a unique dynasty – a dynasty which both ended with Christ's death and also began there as the root of the Christian family.

*"Let your
father and
mother
be glad;
And let her
who bore
you rejoice"*
PROVERBS 23: 25

Birth of Mary

I N the Book of James, Joachim is described as 'exceeding rich' and from one of the twelve tribes of Israel. His wealth is confirmed by his sacrifice of ten lambs and twelve 'tender' calves plus a present to the people of a hundred kids when Anne eventually becomes pregnant. According to the same source, unlike her daughter, but like her cousin Elizabeth, Anne does not conceive until she is old and only after she has beseeched God to take pity on her.

An angel heralds Mary's birth with words that echo the Annunciation. "Anne, Anne," the angel is supposed to have said, "the Lord hath hearkened unto thy prayer thou shalt conceive and bear and thy seed shall be spoken of in the whole world." Anne answers, "As the Lord my God liveth, if I bring forth either male or female child, I will bring it for a gift unto the Lord my God." According to this record, Mary was always recognised as having a great destiny and for that reason was given to the temple at the age of three until she became twelve when she was betrothed to Joseph.

This austere childhood is generally considered very unlikely. The traditional view is that Mary grew up as an ordinary little Jewish girl, possessing, almost certainly, two exceptionally devoted parents. And yet stories about Mary's distinction from an early age have a psychological conviction. The girl who could accept the angel's message with such immediate conviction must have shown signs of a special strength of character.

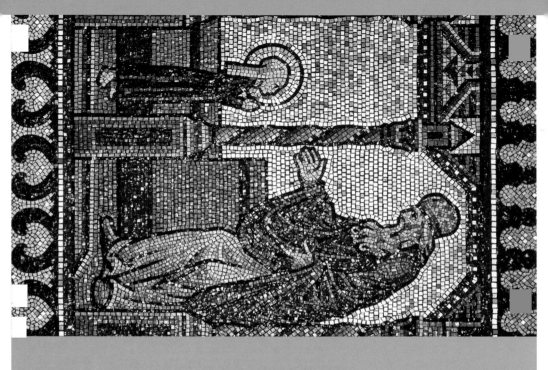

"Mary
Immaculate,
Merely
a woman, yet
Whose
presence
power is
Great as no
Goddess's
Was deemed,
dreamed; who
This one work
had to do"

GERARD MANLEY
HOPKINS

Presentation of Mary in the Temple

MARY, according to the Book of James and Jewish practice, was presented to the temple at the age of three. In James's description, the priest receives her and kisses her and, after making a welcoming speech, invites her to sit upon the third step of the altar. He continues: "And the Lord put grace upon her and she danced with her feet and all the house of Israel loved her." This is an appealing image of a cheerful little girl, not weighed down by any of the great events and sadness in store for her. It makes a good antidote to the more lugubrious images of Christian history. In my mind it is linked with the famous light-heartedness of St Francis who loved to sing and dance and took pleasure in the animals and birds and flowers around him. He, also, of course, wrote the famous paean of praise: "Praise to thee, my Lord for all thy creatures. Above all Brother Sun. Who brings us the Day and lends us his Light...."

Since Mary is to compose one of the great poems of history, the Magnificat, it seems reasonable to suppose that she was not only a thoughtful girl but also imaginative and open to the beauty around her.

"God lent his
paradise to
Joseph's care.
Wherein he
was to plant
the tree of life;
His son, of
Joseph's child
the title bare"

St Robert Southwell.
1595

Mary's betrothal to Joseph

JOSEPH is sometimes called the "silent saint" because he isn't given a line of dialogue in any of the four Gospels. Again, James, in the Apocrypha, produces all sorts of forceful tales, including the much debated information that Joseph had already been married with children and that at first he refused to take the twelve year old Mary as his bride, protesting that he was too old.

I have never been drawn to the "old" image of Mary's husband, as if he were more a grandfather to her or a kind of caretaker whose manliness was in the past or not relevant. Happily, the Joseph of the Lady Chapel is a handsome man in the prime of life — the right sort of man to take the difficult kind of decisions and the vigorous action needed to preserve the lives of his wife and her son in the first years of marriage.

In biblical terms, virginity, as opposed to sterility, set a woman apart, as one chosen for a special role. The Vatican Council Document puts it this way: "This union of the Mother with the Son in the work of salvation is made manifest from the time of Christ's virginal conception up to His death. It is shown first of all when Mary, arising in haste to go to visit Elizabeth, is greeted by her as blessed because of her belief in the promise of salvation and the precursor leaped with joy in the womb of his mother. This union is manifest also at the birth of Our Lord, who did not diminish his mother's virginal integrity but sanctified it." Sometimes, it is seen as an anti-feminist or anti-female condition imposed on a woman by men. But the same men also ordained celibacy for men, for priests — at least in the Roman Catholic strand of Christianity. In fact there is quite a strong argument for seeing Mary as a feminist wife whose vocation, given to her at the Annunciation defines the kind of marriage she has with her husband.

"He will be great, and will be called the Son of the Most High…"

LUKE 1:32

Annunciation by the Angel Gabriel

I N the past, this moving and dramatic scene has been presented as an example of Mary's submissive nature. Now, all the emphasis is on the free decision Mary took to accept the Angel's word and the word of God.

Even forty years ago the report of the Second Vatican Council includes this paragraph: 'The Fathers see Mary not merely as passively engaged by God, but as freely co-operating in the work of man's salvation through faith and obedience." At this stage the "obedience" is still emphasised but in later commentaries the words used more often are: "Faith, hope and love."

One of the ideas that interests me is summed up in another Vatican II phrase, "Death through Eve, life through Mary." It raises all sorts of difficult questions about the first woman's responsibility for the fall of man – here meaning all humanity – but it also puts woman firmly

centre stage, although not, of course, as the leading player. To quote Vatican II once more Mary is described as having "a place in the church which is the highest after Christ and also closest to us."

For me, it is this link both to us and to God, so beautifully expressed in the endless glorious paintings on the Annunciation, which is both moving and uplifting. Mary is one of us, apparently an ordinary Jewish girl, who has enough courage and determination to accept unreservedly a very frightening future. Unlike Zachariah who receives the Angel's news of his elderly wife's pregnancy with understandable doubt, Mary only hesitates until she is in command of the facts. As soon as she understands what is asked of her, she replies, "Behold, I am the handmaid of the Lord; let it be to me according to your word."

Surely no hero has ever shown more courage.

"Blessed are you among women and blessed is the fruit of your womb"

LUKE 1: 39

Visitation of Mary to her cousin, Elizabeth

ERE is Mary at her most independent. Three months pregnant, an unmarried mother, she travels across the spring-green hills of Galilee to visit her cousin, Elizabeth, who is also expecting a baby in mysterious circumstances. This has always seemed the most obviously human of the episodes in Mary's life. It encourages one to imagine all sorts of possibilities, that she is nervous of how Joseph will take the startling news or indeed how her friends and relatives will react. What about her mother, Anne, for example? In the Apocrypha, the priests in the temple are reported as being absolutely horrified that their own very special virgin should be despoiled.

Such fantasies are dispelled instantly by the atmosphere of the meeting between the cousins. They are both overflowing with joy, making it clear that they have come together not timidly to bring each other comfort but to celebrate the wonder of the new births. Mary's emotions burst out with that great hymn of praise, The Magnificat, which comes as fresh off the page as if it had just been composed: "My soul magnifies the Lord; and my spirit rejoices in God my Saviour..." Every happily expectant mother since feels an echo of her beautiful words. In the nature of things, new birth, new life, casts a glow over the whole world, whatever the circumstances.

It is sometimes seen as strange that Mary doesn't stay with Elizabeth longer, perhaps through the birth of St John. But their meeting and recognition of each other's remarkable fortune lifts their story out of the everyday at the same time as it makes them seem like two women sharing the bond of pregnancy.

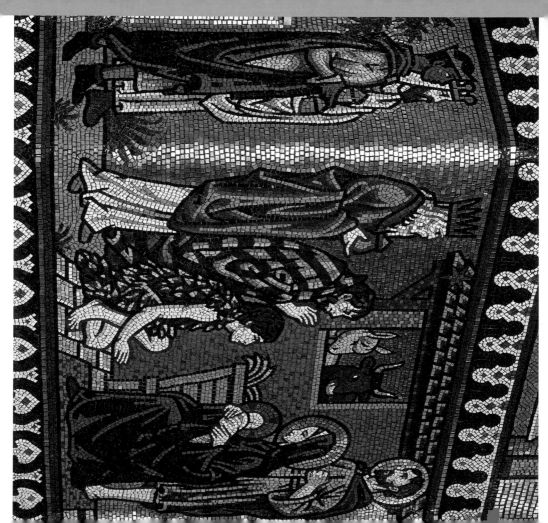

Nativity at Bethlehem

S AINT Francis was the first to present the nativity scene as a time and place for Christians to worship. Knowing so well the nature of suffering, he also appreciated the happiness that such worship could bring. The descriptions in Luke and Matthew are romantic enough for the ingredients of any fabulous tale: the young woman uprooted from home at the time when she would most like to be calm; the baby born in a cave or stable; the angels appearing to the shepherd and the star catching the attention of three kings far away to the east. The scene never loses its power to enthrall and instruct.

But what of Mary herself? The birth of Jesus and his early years are filled with difficulties and dangers. And yet virtually all the thousands of portraits, icons and statues of Mary and the Christ child created over two thousand years, show a calm, proud mother. The clue to Mary, the composed and confident mother, perhaps comes from the few words, almost asides when she is described as "retaining everything in her heart." She is capable of focusing on what is most important in her life without being distracted by local problems in the company, moreover, of an assortment of animals and some very ungrand peasants smelling of sheep.

There are a few girlish-looking portraits of Mary in which the sun shines and her golden hair tumbles over her pretty shoulders. But to me the most convincing are the far more serious pictures, reflecting the dignity of her new position as the mother of God.

"And she gave birth to her first-born son and wrapped Him in swaddling cloths and laid Him in a manger; because there was no place for them in the inn"

LUKE 2: 7

"Behold this child is set for the fall and rise of many in Israel, (and a sword shall pierce through your own soul also)"

LUKE 2: 34-35

Presentation of Jesus in the Temple

BABIES are almost always a source of celebration and joy. Yet Luke uses the presentation of Jesus in the temple as an occasion to bring home how his birth cannot be separated from future suffering. The sword that will pierce Mary's side seems doubly cruel, almost against nature, on such a day of celebration. Anyone who has been involved in a baby's baptism – and at Easter 2003 my oldest grandson was baptised in the Lady Chapel – knows what an extraordinary feeling it is to be bringing new life to a religious centre and ask for him or her to be made part of a community of souls.

Jesus's presentation (which also encompassed Mary's purification according to Jewish custom) took place nearly three decades before St John the Baptist received people on the banks of the River Jordan. But Mary must have felt the same sort of blessed pride as any mother or even grandmother. What a misfortune, therefore, to have the ancient Simeon, prophet of doom, who, not content with recognising and hailing the Saviour, cannot resist predicting the ghastly suffering which will come to Mary through her son. He seems almost like the wicked fairy in the tale of Sleeping Beauty who casts her spell over the innocent baby.

As often in Mary's story, our human wish to enjoy a simple moment of happiness has been moved onto another plane. Jesus's divinity has made sure that his mother's experience was altogether different from expected. Simeon, an exceptionally holy – not wicked – priest, has recognised him for what he is and his tribute brings lasting hope as well as human suffering. An ordinary event on the human calendar has become extraordinary.

Flight into Egypt

*"Rise...
and flee...
for Herod is
about to search
for the child"*

MATTHEW 2: 13

ARY, the exile, the asylum-seeker, is a powerful image. A mother and small child could not walk all the way to Egypt, so the donkey – perhaps the same that took them to Bethlehem – appears and at its side the stalwart figure of Joseph. This is the moment when Joseph takes control of his family's life. The Angel has appeared to him, not to Mary, and given his instructions. Jesus's life will be saved and our imagination switches back to the appalling massacre of those babies and little boys who had no angel to warn their parents and will die a gruesome death.

Yet the fate of the family fleeing into the unknown was certainly not enviable. Egypt was an alien land to them; they could not know if King Herod's spies would seek them out nor could they guess that he would die in a relatively short time. This unsettled period in the lives of Mary and Joseph sometimes seems to pass seamlessly into what we assume to be the tranquil life at Nazareth with the consequence that its significance to the family is not fully recognised. In my imagination, the Egyptian episode is the time when the family become truly bound together, becoming the Holy Family, cut off, as they were, from their friends and relatives.

Mary, through this experience, is provided with a personal link to the long line of exiles who continue to this day.

Finding in the Temple

"...and all who heard him were amazed at his understanding and his answers... and his mother said to Him, 'Son why have you treated us so?'"

LUKE 2: 47-48

THIS is the first occasion when Jesus seems to be treating his mother badly. It is a vivid, well-constructed report with its lesson pointed out by Jesus himself: "Did you not know that I must be in my father's house?" He is reminding his mother at this important stage in his life – time for Bar Mitzvah for a Jewish boy and confirmation for Christians – that He is only with her for a finite period, lent to her, as it were by God. In this scale of things, her extreme anxiety has no place.

The human side of the event remains real to us, however, echoing the innumerable occasions when mothers watch their children grow up and move into the dangerous world outside the protection of the home. Jesus's parents behaved exactly as any loving and sensible parents would, worrying over their fledgling falling out of the nest before He is ready to fly.

The surprise, following Jesus's explanation of the position, lies in the two subsequent sentences in which He is described as returning to Nazareth and "being obedient to them" while Mary, in one of those great understated phrases "kept all these things in her heart." This is the accepting role which most mothers of a runaway twelve year old would find both impossible and inappropriate.

"And Jesus increased in wisdom and in stature and in favour with God and man"

LUKE 2: 52

Home at Nazareth

THE Apocryphal Gospels of St James and St Thomas are remarkably inventive about Jesus's boyhood. With a logic based, presumably, on his later ministry, they describe Him as headstrong and prone to bring out a miracle when crossed. They have an almost sacrilegious feel to them, particularly when set alongside the traditional image of Jesus as the little boy helping his father in the carpenter's shop. At one point in St Thomas' Gospel, Jesus makes his detractors blind which infuriates Joseph "who took hold on him by his ear in anger" at which Jesus retorts furiously, ending, "Albeit I am with thee now, yet I was made before thee."

There are more attractive anecdotes too: Jesus makes twelve sparrows out of clay and when his tell-tale friends complain to Joseph that it's the Sabbath, Jesus commands the sparrow to fly away – who do so merrily, praising almighty God. On another occasion, asked by Mary to bring water from the well, He finds himself without bucket and, undeterred, brings the water back in his cloak. Such stories which sometimes elicit blame and sometimes respect or even veneration from his peers or elders, dramatically fill in the years before the New Testament takes up his story.

Although essentially unverified, it is tempting to link them to Jesus's problems when He returns to Nazareth during his ministry and so angers the inhabitants that He escapes being thrown over a cliff, only by using his miraculous powers. This, linked with the famous comment: "Nothing good comes out of Nazareth," has tended to put the blame on the unpleasant nature of the Nazarenes. But maybe Jesus himself had left behind a reputation for perversity. Both the description of the finding in the temple and the marriage feast at Cana suggest that He was, at very least, outspoken.

So it seems to me credible that Mary found herself not only the mother of God but also of a remarkable but difficult child who was preparing himself for his extraordinary future. If this were the case, Mary's role would be both more demanding and more rewarding.

Marriage Feast at Cana

"When the wine failed, the mother of Jesus said to Him, 'They have no wine.' And Jesus said to her, 'Oh woman, what have you to do with me?'"

JOHN 2: 3-4

SAINT John gives us this story with a feeling of intimacy and it is often supposed that he was present. The conventional argument as to whether Jesus was actually being rude to his mother continues but it has always perfectly clear to me that however posterity might judge his words, Mary herself was neither insulted nor surprised. Her calm order to the servants, "Do whatever He tells you." shows complete confidence in her son's intention to comply with her request.

The relationship between a mother and a son is one of the most discussed in psychology. Since Freud's work, it is usually interpreted in terms of sex, but also of gender. As Jesus's mission in the world did not include an active sex life – although He didn't hold back from airing his views on the subject – it is in the area of gender that the relationship is worth studying. Clearly, we are looking at a time when women were generally not considered the equal of men in any sphere of life except the home and even then the man was head of the household. Nevertheless it is Mary who, according to John's report, is given the job of propelling her son, already at thirty a mature man, into the wider world.

This is an extraordinary act of deference by Jesus to his mother and therefore to woman in general. His attitude here is born out by all the subsequent years of his life on earth when, within the code of the time – and sometimes stretching it quite a bit – He allows women to be participants in his journey. I have always believed this showed the influence of a strong mother, his first example of a woman and the most essential.

"Truly I say to you, no prophet is a prophet in his own country"

LUKE 4: 24

Mary bids farewell to Jesus at the start of his Ministry

IT must have been at Capernum, a town on the shores of the Lake of Galilee that Jesus said goodbye to Mary. The country through which He travelled and preached was small enough so that, even on foot, He was never very far from his mother and she may well have been among "the women" often described in the Gospels as being present on one occasion or another. So the farewell is less about a physical separation than a total dedication to a new way of life – which will, eventually, lead to suffering and death. We do know that she was present at a tricky moment when He is in danger of being crushed by the crowds because both Mark and Luke report it in similar words. But when told of his mother's arrival, together with "his brethren", He asks, "Who are my mother and my brothers?" and, looking round at those sitting around Him supplies the plain answer,

"Whoever does the will of God is my brother and sister and mother."

By now Mary must have had more hints than Simeon's about the sword that is to pierce her side. One assumes that, like any mother of a son committing himself to heroic deeds, she is filled with fear but also with pride. The pride, of course, depends on her belief in the cause which He has espoused. The plight of the mother who sees her son fighting in a war or for a cause in which she cannot believe is truly pitiable. The mother of a grown-up son has already given everything of importance as He is growing up and now is helpless to alter his decision.

Mary's position as mother of God has meant that she has never known better than her son. Her faith in his unalterable rightness was fixed at the time of the Annunciation. This faith will gradually spread through the rest of Jesus's disciples.

Way of the Cross

"So they took Jesus and He went out, bearing his own cross to the place called the place of a skull, which in Hebrew is Golgotha"

JOHN 19: 17

THE abrupt transition in this cycle from Jesus setting out hopefully on his ministry to Jesus bent under the cross on which He is to die is very shocking. Three years have passed but we are shown none of his triumphs, no gathering of thousands to hear his teaching, no dramatic entry into Jerusalem when palm branches are thrown adoringly under his feet by the very same people who are to condemn Him to be crucified.

There is no specific mention of Mary during Jesus' final journey towards death until his very last hours on earth. But the certainty of her presence then and Luke's reference to "women who lamented him" makes her presence earlier seem extremely likely. The soldier guarding Jesus keeps a firm hold on his tunic as if afraid of the sight of his mother might cause him to break free.

But both Mary and Jesus know his fate cannot be altered – even though Jesus himself is at times faint-hearted. The veneration of Mary has been at various times suspect to different forms of Christianity and, it goes without saying to other religions. It was feared that, particularly among the uneducated who found it easier to pray to a woman and mother than a being far beyond any comprehension as God, she was being elevated above her proper station. After the reformation in England, there was a loss of ancient Marian devotion. Yet she retains her place in the church not only as Jesus's mother but as his first and most faithful disciple.

'When Jesus saw his mother, and the disciple whom He loved standing near, he said to his mother, 'Woman, behold your son!' Then he said to the disciple, 'Behold your mother!' '

JOHN 19: 26

Crucifixion

IT is easy to identify with the human story of a mother who watches her son, still in the prime of life, tortured and then murdered. Over the centuries women have suffered an equivalent agony to that suffered by their sons. Most often, in war or civilian accident or violence, the mother won't be actually present but will live through it afterwards in her imagination. But Mary stood at the foot of the cross as the last terrible and wonderful act of Jesus's life unfolded. By her presence there she represents the mother of sorrows all over the world and through time. It is an unforgettable image and one that has brought consolation to many.

By the time Christ died, He had warned his disciples many times that He would have to leave them in order to complete his mission on earth. But in the event, this hardly seemed to give them extra courage. But Mary's faith has always seemed of a special order, totally certain, without drama and also without doubt. So it would be nice to think that, unlike the men, she was sustained by a belief in the Resurrection to come. Yet we who watch the scene with full knowledge of the glories to follow still find ourselves shocked by the brutality of Jesus's death. Perhaps it is a measure of our ties to this world.

> "Safe is your
> living Son who
> has power over
> the four seasons:
> winter, spring,
> bright-visaged
> summer,
> autumn with
> its fruits..."
>
> BLATHMAC C 700 AD

News of the resurrection is

THE story of Christ's resurrection is dominated by women, even though the Gospels record slightly different versions of the same events. In Luke's Gospel, there are three women, not two. In John's Gospel, Mary Magdalen first goes to find Peter and John and then sees Jesus whom she mistakes initially for a gardener. None of them, however, mentions Mary, the mother of

brought to Mary by Peter and John

Jesus. The designer of the Lady Chapel cycle makes the logical supposition that Peter and, in particular John, into whose care Mary has been placed by her son, would tell Mary the extraordinary news as quickly as possible. One can imagine the mourning Mary, almost certainly a widow and, although probably not yet fifty, an older woman by the standards of those times, waiting quietly on the side-lines.

When the news of her son's escape from the tomb is brought to Mary, she becomes the first mother to be saved from everlasting mourning by a belief in life after death.

"Lady so great and powerful – he who seeks grace apart from thee flies without wings"

DANTE PARADISO
CANTO 33
(WORDS OF
ST BERNARD)

Descent of the Holy Spirit at Pentecost

MARY presides at the centre of the gathered apostles, the focal point of the scene. After her son's death she is needed to help found the church that is being started in His name. Most importantly, the Holy Spirit – here depicted as tongues of fire – has come to her already when the Angel announced that she would be the virgin mother of God, "Hail Mary, full of grace, blessed art thou amongst women..." She is the link between the opening of the drama of Jesus's life on earth and the first scene of the new drama of his church. One of her titles, "Mother of the Church" recognises this truth.

This moment of grace descending is perhaps not only a return to the Annunciation but also a forecast of the time when Mary will sit among the saints in heaven, at her son's right hand, honoured in majesty as Queen of Heaven.

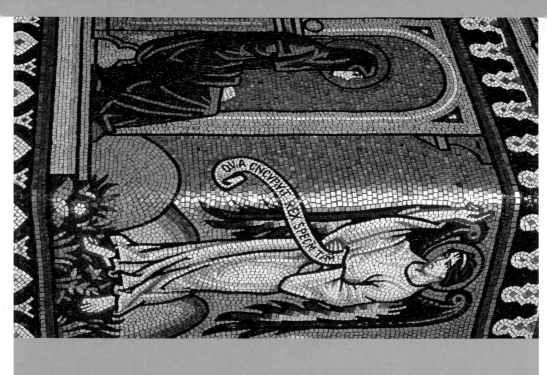

"Suffer us not
to mock
ourselves with
falsehood.
Teach us how
to care and
not to care.
Teach us to
sit still.
Even among
these rocks"

T S ELIOT
ASH WEDNESDAY

Angel predicts the death of Mary

I T seems fitting that the Angel Gabriel should come to Mary to tell her of her death, just as he came to announce the birth of Jesus. There are moving descriptions in several different writings of the Apocrypha. In most of them Mary begs to be allowed to avoid the terrors of hell which, to a modern mind, seems a rather unnecessary fear. In the Pseudo-Melito, the Angel carries a glowing palm while he reassures her, 'The power of hell shall not hurt thee; but an eternal blessing hath the Lord thy God given thee, of whom I am the servant and messenger; but think not that the power not to see the prince of Darkness can be but by him whom thou didst bear in thy womb for his is all power, world without end given by me.'

There has always been uneasiness in the Church about how to approach the continuing life and death of the mother of God. This culminated in the doctrine of the Assumption that allowed Mary to bypass ordinary mortality and make her way directly to sit by her son in heaven. However, although the Immaculate Conception was declared dogma in 1854, it was nearly a hundred years later that Pope Pius XII formally declared the Assumption an article of faith.

The Lady Chapel imagery reflects generations of devotion. Mary sits in a resigned, very human manner, hands clasped in her lap and the Angel, instead of carrying a brilliant palm, holds a banner on which these poetic words are written in Latin: "The King requires your beauty.'

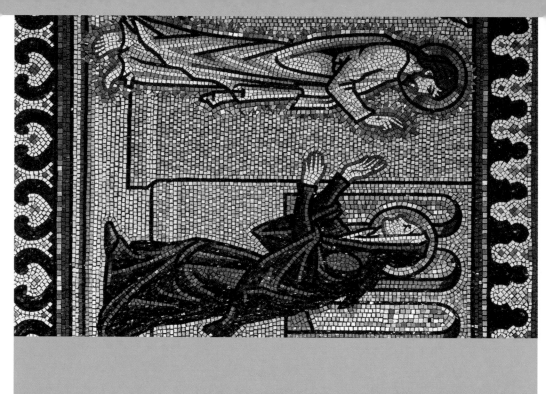

"Then the
Saviour spoke,
saying: 'Come,
thou most
precious pearl,
enter in the
treasury of
eternal life'"

LATIN NARRATIVE
OF PSEUDO-MELITO
FROM THE APOCRYPHAL
NEW TESTAMENT

Risen Jesus appears to his Mother

BEREAVED wife, husband, mother, father or close friend will frequently report seeing the dead beloved as if he or she is truly present. It is as if the spirit is still lingering in the space around those who have been left behind. Gradually, as time passes, the visitations become less frequent and the mourning process moves to another phase. So often, Christ's story and the story of Mary records a supernatural happening which aligns with a human reality. It is what makes the Gospels as accessible to a child as a theologian.

In fact, only in the Apocrypha is there any suggestion that Jesus did revisit his mother at the end of her life. Clearly, the designer of the pictorial biography felt the rightness of the idea, as if Jesus were personally summoning his mother to join Him in heaven, signalling her release from this world and her entry into the next.

Dormition of Mary

T HE traditional image of Mary's death (dormition) is always peaceful. We – at least those of us who inhabit the Western world – live to ever greater ages, Mary's tranquillity at the end seems more and more desirable: her experiences have ranged from the terrifyingly wonderful to the terrifyingly dreadful. In the last fifty years the hospice movement has recognised the importance of dying with dignity. It is understood how hard it is to find inner peace in a hospital where the emphasis, however caring, is on the needs of the body. We have no real idea how or when Mary's life ended but it is impossible to believe that the faith and strength she showed in her life would desert her in her parting. Those who live well, die well.

Mary's importance in the church continued after her Assumption into heaven, at first with a special worship in the Eastern churches. The early 20th century when the Lady Chapel cycle was conceived, was a period of intense Marian piety. Since the middle of the nineteenth century there had been appearances at, for example, Lourdes, Fatima, Guadalupe and Knock. All are visited by hundreds and thousands of pilgrims every year. Miracles continue to be claimed, despite few ever passing through the rigorous vetting process. More important, pilgrims, sick or healthy, return home re-invigorated in body or mind. To many the rosary is a life-long way of prayer. Others say her prayer, the Hail Mary, with a fervent hope of intercession to her son or because she, herself, is an inspiration for the Christian way of faith, hope and love.

Thus Mary's spirit of determined service lives on.

*"Hark!
She is call'd.
The parting
hour is come.
Take thy
farewell, poor
world. Heav'n
must go home"*

RICHARD CRASHAW
1649

Saint Luke writing the Gospel

IT is only in St Luke's Gospel that we have a full account of the Annunciation, the account of Mary's visit to Elizabeth and of the visits to Jerusalem. There is even the serious suggestion that the first two chapters of Luke, so Hebrew in their outlook, although he himself was a Greek, were actually written by Mary or at least with her assistance. He was not beloved of Jesus as St John nor was Mary given to him as a special charge but he was the supreme recorder, continuing in the role as St Paul's secretary. Without Luke's Gospels, Mary's story would be more fragmentary and less colourful.

Just as appositely, Luke is the patron saint of painters so he has a double reason to be represented in the final panel of this series. Furthermore, there is a tradition that he painted from life the "Black Madonna" at Jasna Gora on a beam from the Holy family's house in Nazareth. St Augustine firmly denied there were any portraits from life of Mary but, whether Luke painted Mary or not, his written descriptions have inspired many magnificent works of art over two thousand years. Our world has been enriched by his record.

Lady Chapel mosaics – a brief history

THE parishioners of St Mary's, Horseferry Road, nervously assembling in the Lady Chapel early on St Joseph's Day 1903 for the first Mass in the Cathedral, would have seen a Chapel very different from that of today. Red cotton hangings hid the recesses and the parishioners had brought the seating, stations of the cross, statues and pulpit from St Mary's, but the Chapel was otherwise unadorned bare brick with just a crucifix above the altar. It was to be five years before everything changed.

First, just before the Eucharistic Congress of 1908, the walls and altar were panelled with a rich variety of marbles. Then came the lovely blue mosaic altarpiece of the Virgin and Child, together with the four blue niche mosaics of Old Testament prophets who foresaw the Incarnation, all designed by the Nonconformist artist, Robert Anning Bell RA and executed by the experienced mosaicist, Gertrude Martin, in 1912-13. But although these mosaics were generally praised, Cardinal Bourne was not satisfied, and he was even more disappointed with Anning Bell's tympanum mosaic above the Cathedral main entrance (executed in 1915-16). In desperation he looked for a Catholic artist with a style more to his own taste.

In 1923 Gilbert Pownall, a Catholic artist whose work had appeared at the Royal Academy, painted a portrait of Cardinal Bourne to celebrate his twenty years as Archbishop. Bourne asked him to design mosaics for the Lady Chapel. In 1927 a model was displayed in Archbishop's House, meeting with "general admiration and approval". Work on the Lady Chapel started in 1930 under Basil Carey-Elwes (pictured left) with two English mosaicists, to be joined by two Venetians a year later. It was to last five years. Against a sea of gold a garland of flowers, representing a rosary, is carried by angels around the Chapel. Below are events associated with Our Lady - the doctrine of the Immaculate Conception, the rosary given to St Dominic, the scapular given to St Simon Stock, and the appearance of Our Lady at Lourdes.

But it is the frieze at the lowest level which is the most appealing. Starting with Our Lady's father and mother (Joachim and Anne) together with King David, it consists of a series of scenes celebrating her life as recorded in both the New Testament (the Annunciation, Visitation etc) and ancient tradition (the gift of the seamless robe, her meeting with the Risen Lord etc). All culminates in the mosaics above the blue altarpiece where Christ reigns in glory at the centre of the Tree of Life. In its branches, amidst the flower garland and elsewhere in the Chapel, are a multitude of animals - over a hundred mammals, birds, butterflies and other insects, of which Pownall's notebooks were full.

At the time, the new mosaics were not universally admired. Both Pownall's iconography and his rather sentimental, Victorian style came in for criticism. More recently the Chapel has been likened to a child's picture-book, and it is this, perhaps, which has made it the most loved in the Cathedral, particularly among children and those who are able to see with the eyes of a child.

Patrick Rogers

A powerful echo of the Orthodox

ORTHODOX Christians, following the tradition of the Apostolic Church, have always retained a deep love and veneration of Mary, the Birthgiver of God (or, Theotokos), and our worship is filled with references to her. Both in this and in our iconography, she is always associated (even if occasionally by implication) with her son, Who (in the words of the Creed): "For our sake and for our salvation came down from heaven, and was incarnate from the Holy Spirit and the Virgin Mary and became man". Indeed, one of the more frequent depictions of the Theotokos - to be found in the apse of Orthodox churches - is that of the Virgin Who is "wider than the heavens" (or, Platytera) and who is hymned as being "the heavenly ladder by which God came down (to earth)" while at the same time being compared to a "ladder raising all from earth by grace".[1]

Meditating on her, a twentieth-century saint, asks: "If God the Father chose her, God the Holy Spirit descended upon her, and God the Son dwelt in her, submitted to her in the days of His youth, was concerned for her when hanging on the cross then should not everyone who confesses the Holy Trinity venerate her?"[2] This is both a challenge and a rationale for all Christians. For us as Orthodox Christians, it justifies our deep love and affection for her whom we see as our common mother and whom we hymn with the most exquisite poetry and whom we depict in brilliant mosaics and radiant icons. And not only this, for our affection for the mother of God extends to the non-religious sphere and suffuses secular art and poetry as well.

In the mosaics of the Lady Chapel of Westminster's Roman Catholic Cathedral, we see a powerful echo of the Orthodox ethos of iconography, with many scenes being immediately recognisable. Here we discern the Nativity of the Mother of God, in which "the Virgin sanctifies the sterile womb of nature and grafts into its fruit essness the fruitfulness of virtue...The Lord's throne is being prepared on earth, earthly things are sanctified, the heavenly hosts are mingled with us."[3] We see, too, Her Entry into the Temple when "the temple that contained God, the Mother of God is...brought into the Lord's Temple, and Zachary receives her."[4a] It is the day when "the Holy of Holies rejoices and the choir of Angels mystically celebrates."[4b] We witness the Salutation of the Archangel Gabriel to Her Who is "full of grace" as he comes "flying from the arches of heaven (to Nazareth to announce) the glad tidings of the Lord's coming"[5] and we hear the Virgin's humble reply (an example to us all as we submit to the Will of God).

A little further on, we observe the Mystery of Christ's Nativity, and rhetorically ask ourselves: "What shall we offer you, O Christ, because you have appeared on earth as a man for our sakes? For each of the creatures made by you offers you its thanks"; and we reply: "The Angels (offer) their hymn; the heavens the star; the shepherds their wonder; the Magi their gifts; the earth the cave; the desert the manger; but we (humanity, in all humility, have the honour and privilege of offering) a Virgin mother.[6] And then our eyes are filled with scenes from the childhood of Christ and the beginning of His ministry.

Subsequently, we see the All-Holy One as she meets her son being led to His crucifixion and we witness her as she stands at the foot of the cross, where "The bridegroom of the church is transfixed with nails (and) the son of the Virgin is pierced by a lance;"[7a] and we remember the hymnographer's words: "When she who bore you saw you hanging on the cross, O Christ," she cried out, "What is this strange mystery that I see, my son? How are you dying on a tree, nailed in the flesh, O giver of life?"[7b] Whom "now as a corpse we see, unsightly, bereft of form".[8]

But, following the death of Christ on the cross, we are ourselves witnesses of His glorious resurrection and, together with St John Chrysostom, we ask, "Where, death, is your sting? Where hell, is your victory?" And we proclaim, "Christ has risen and you (death and hell) are abolished! Christ has risen and the demons have fallen! Christ has risen, and Angels rejoice! Christ has risen, and life has found freedom! Christ has risen, and there is no corpse in the grave! For Christ, being raised from the dead, has become the first fruits of those who sleep."[9] And, together with the Virgin and all creation, we rejoice, sharing in the light and joy of the resurrection.

But, as Christ promised, His Church was not left comfortless; and, fifty days after His resurrection, God the Father sent the Paraclete to abide with it for ever (cf John 14:16 & 26). As the hymnographer declares: "Marvellous things all the nations saw today in the city of David, when the Holy Spirit came down in tongues of fire, as Luke, God's mouthpiece, declared. For he said, when Christ's disciples were assembled, there came a sound as of a mighty wind, and filled the whole house where they were sitting; and all began to speak with strange words, strange doctrines, strange teachings of the Holy Trinity."[10] And here, enthroned among the disciples, we see her who gave birth to Him and whom the early Church held in the highest honour and Who was an unceasing inspiration to the apostles.

Furthermore, sacred tradition teaches us that Christ's all-holy mother was accustomed to leave her temporal home on Mount Sion and ascend the Mount of Olives to pray at a place (today marked by a chapel) near to where her son had returned to the heavens. But when the time came for her to return to her heavenly home, the Archangel Gabriel was sent "by divine command" to announce to her that the time of her translation was at hand. And thus, after three days, she fell asleep, with "clouds (catching) the apostles up into the air; and though they were scattered through the world, made them form a single choir in the presence of (her) most pure body. As they reverently buried (her in the venerable tomb that's venerated to this day in Gethsemane), they sang Gabriel's song, crying out: "Hail, full of grace, Virgin Mother without bridegroom, the Lord is with you."[11]

As is well-known, Orthodox Christians use many expressions of endearment when speaking of Christ's mother, chief among these being that of "Panaghia" (which may be translated as the "All-Holy One"). This emphasises the uniqueness of her contribution to the mission of Christ and the singleness of her role in human history (and it is this which we see depicted and stressed in these mosaics in the Lady Chapel). But not only this. Orthodox faithful understand the term "Panaghia" as including an intimacy as well as something which is beyond our comprehension and which encompasses the "mystery" of her participation in the economy of God for humanity. And this understanding reaches to the heart of even the humblest of Christians.

We, therefore, share with our forefathers in the faith in praising her whom we hymn as being "Greater in honour than the Cherubim and beyond compare more glorious than the Seraphim" since it is she who "without corruption…gave birth to God the Word" and it is she who is indeed "truly the Mother of God"[12] and mother of us all.

† Αρχιεπίσκοπος Θυατείρων καὶ Μ. Βρετανίας

Gregorios, Archbishop of Thyateira and Great Britain

1. The Akathist Hymn | 2. St John Maximovitch in: The Orthodox Veneration of Mary The Birthgiver of God | 3. St Photius the Great in: Homily on the Birth of the Virgin | 4 a-b. Vespers of the Forefeast of the Entry of the Mother of God | 5. St Photius the Great in: Homily on the Annunciation | 6. Great Vespers of Christmas | 7a-b. Matins of Great Friday | 8. The Encomia of Matins of Great Saturday | 9. The Catechetical Sermon of St John Chrysostom, read after Matins on Easter night | 10. Lauds of the Feast of Pentecost | 11. Lauds of the Feast of the Dormition | 12. A Hymn of the Orthodox Church, frequently used during the Divine Liturgy

An aid to devotion

I have walked down the aisles of Westminster Cathedral on a number of occasions. That is a source of astonishment and joy to me for I am a Methodist and an ordained minister. When I was at school it was forbidden, for me to say the Lord's Prayer in the same room with my Catholic friends but in recent years I have been given a seat of honour on special occasions and have even preached in the Cathedral. But on none of these occasions did I notice the mosaics in the Lady Chapel. They are noticeable only if your attention is drawn to them and you are prepared to gaze heavenward.

So having been invited to offer a contribution to this book, I went to look at the originals. I stood in the Lady Chapel turning on my heels and craning my neck. A number of other people were also in the Chapel, saying their prayers with eyes closed or cast down, or contemplating the altar. I looked my fill and turned away. I glanced back and saw a number of the people there were now standing up to see what had attracted my attention.

I hope this book of photographs will work in the same way. That it will encourage others to see what might otherwise have gone unnoticed.

It seems to me that that was much the purpose of the mosaics themselves. The last one portrays the evangelist Luke writing - a recognition that it is Luke's account of the good news of Jesus that more than the other Gospels draws the attention to the person of Mary, the mother of our Lord.

The mosaics call upon Scripture and tradition to tell the story of the woman who offered her body and her blood to enable the greater offering that would change the world's understanding of God's relationship with his people.

The mosaics are fresh and clear and very beautiful and this book of photographs captures them well. There are wonderful touches and I suppose each one who looks will see those things that inspire them. The depiction of a special Resurrection appearance to Mary while it may not be Scriptural - I really want it to have happened in this way. And as to the tongues of flame sitting on the heads of Mary and the disciples at Pentecost - that image will make me giggle to myself for some time.

The story of the wedding at Cana is included in the mosaics. Here is a Biblical story where Mary draws attention to her son and says, "Do what he tells you." It echoes the voice of God at the Baptism and Transfiguration, "This is my son listen to him." Many (including not a few Methodists!) have found that giving attention to the person of Mary has sustained them in discipleship. I hope this book will prove to be an aid to devotion as well as an artistic delight.

The Reverend Baroness Richardson of Callow OBE
Former Moderator of the Free Churches Group

A woman of the House of Imran

MARY the Mother of Jesus as the Ideal of Motherhood in Islam Mary, Mariam in the Qur'an, the mother of Jesus is mentioned more than thirty times in the Holy Qur'an. Sura (chapter) 19 of the Qur'an is named after her. The Qur'an relates her life story from its beginning by stating that her mother, a woman of the House of Imran, when pregnant prayed to God saying:

"O Lord I offer You what I carry in my womb in dedication to Your service. Accept it from me for You are All-Hearing and All-Knowing." But when she had given birth to the child she said: "O Lord I have given birth to a female," - the while God had been fully aware of what she would give birth to and fully aware that no male child (she might have hoped for) could ever have been like this female - "and I have named her Mary and I seek Your protection for her and her offspring from Satan, the accursed."

And her Lord accepted her with goodly acceptance and caused her to grow up with excellence and placed her in the care of Zachariah. Whenever Zachariah visited her in the sanctuary, he found her provided with food. He would ask: "O Mary where did this come from?" She would answer: "It is from God; God gives food in abundance to whomever He wills." Sura 3 verses 36-38

The exalted position of Mary in Islam is expressed in the Qur'anic verses 42-43, Sura: The angels said: "O Mary! Behold, God has elected you and made you immaculate, and raised you above all women of the world. So Mary remain truly devoted to your Lord and prostrate yourself in worship and bow down with those who bow down (before Him)."

With this quality Mary was thus prepared for the great and noble task of being the mother of Jesus, whose conception, birth and career would demand the utmost devotion, affection and support. Her experience of joy and pain, of bafflement and pride is expressed in the following Qur'anic verses:

The angels said: "O Mary! Behold, God sends you the glad tidings of a word from Him (of a son) who shall be close to Him and he shall speak to the people in his cradle and as a grown man and shall be of the righteous." Sura 3 verses 42-46

The motherhood of Mary is detailed in Sura 19 verses 16-36. It begins thus:

"And call to mind, through this divine book (the Qur'an), Mary when she withdrew to an eastern place and kept herself in seclusion from her people whereupon We sent Our angel of revelation to her who appeared to her in the shape of a perfectly shaped human being. She exclaimed: "Verily I seek refuge from you in the Merciful. [Approach me not] if you are conscious of Him."

[The angel answered]: "I am a messenger of God to bestow upon you the gift of a son endowed with purity." She said: "How can I have a son when no man has ever touched me? - For never have I been a loose woman." [The angel said]: "This is the order of your Lord Who said it is easy for Me to do and (you shall have a son) so that We might make him a symbol to humankind and an act of grace from Us." And it was a thing already decreed. Verses 16 – 21.

When the son was born, Mary, carrying him in her arms, came upon her people. They gathered around her and accused her of having committed a shocking deed. "You of the House of Aaron, your father was not a wicked man nor was your mother a loose woman."

She pointed to the infant, who exonerated his mother from the accusation levelled against her. From the moment of the birth of the Christ Jesus, Mary's life was totally absorbed into the life and career of her son. During his short ministry she shared in his troubles and tribulations She was and remains the model for womanhood and motherhood.

Sheikh Dr M A Zaki Badawi
Chairman, Muslim Council of Great Britain

In the House of Life - a personal reflection

Ma never told her boss she was pregnant. It was 1930, a slump year, and Dad was looking for a job because no one could afford a bespoke tailor, especially when you could now get a ready-made suit for 40 shillings. So to keep her job, Ma concealed everything, ie me. But she couldn't conceal her centre of gravity, which was steadily shifting, and all was revealed when she made a misjudged leap off a tram and was promptly taken by ambulance to the Salvation Army Hospital in Hackney, where I was born in record time.

I did not at first find favour with Ma, as I emerged cocooned in black hair and very cross. Ma only liked blondies, which is why she didn't like rabbis with long black beards, but drooled over clean-cut Mormon missionaries. She never listened to them, she said. She only liked to gaze at them.

When she examined me, she said, shocked: "My God, it's the devil!" whereupon her mother (my Bubbe) snatched me from her, saying I was an angel, and my mother was no Yiddishe Momme to say such things. Oh yes she was, replied Ma weakly. My granny said she wasn't. Ma said defiantly she was and Dad had to snatch me away while the other women in the ward cheered both sides on. They didn't have much cheer in their lives, poor things, as Ma was the only married woman in the ward and so got special treatment.

Was she a Yiddishe Momme? The question worried her. It was the weak point in her armour, and later on I learnt how to exploit it. She certainly worked her fingers to the bone for Dad and me and she gave away her only winter coat to our coughing cleaning woman. She also braved the bombs and the ack-ack every other

"I sat on a bench nearly to await events. Sure enough, her personality and her words invaded my mind"

night during the Blitz to visit my dying uncle in hospital. But there was a streak of irreverence and levity in her which torpedoed her sporadic sallies into piety.

These thoughts ran through my mind last week as I visited her grave on her "Yahrzeit" – the anniversary of her death. After intoning the memorial prayers and purloining a pebble from a neighbouring grave (Abraham marked Sarah's resting place with a stone), I sat on a bench nearby to await events. Sure enough, her personality and her words invaded my mind. "I wouldn't come out here again, Lionel" she sniffed. "I've got my own journey and it's time to cut that umbilical cord. You should be dancing the night away in Benidorm, not moping among all this marble junk. What you've done, Lionel, you've done, and the rest is gravy."

It was a curious offbeat Sybilline remark, but upbeat, and I've been pondering it. The only tombstone she ever admired was one featuring a larger than lifesize marble youngster, looking intent astride a marble motorbike.

I didn't bring any flowers to leave on Ma's grave. She didn't really like real ones, they were too much trouble, only plastic ones, brightly coloured like boiled sweets. It was too late to find one of those, so in addition to the pebble, I purloined an only slightly wilting long-stemmed red baccarat rose from an unregarded pile and put it on her stone as a romantic gesture. Though she would have giggled, she would have liked it.

Ma did not take kindly to my becoming a rabbi. She had slaved for years to get me out of the ghetto, and here I was jumping right

> "She had taught me real religion which is 'generosity of spirit'. I miss her, my not quite but more than Yiddishe Momme"

back into it again. Was I going to grow a fuzzy beard? But after I reassured her that I would remain clean-shaven, she was mollified and became quite interested in my studies.

"Will all that religion you learn at the seminary make you nice?" she asked over our curry and pink gin. I decided to match her honesty. "I don't know" I answered. "I think mine makes me nicer, but we'll have to wait and see." I think this was the most important spiritual question anybody ever asked me. In religion as in everything else, you have to discriminate. Third-rate religion is dangerous stuff, as is only too obvious from the pages of our newspapers.

Now some rabbis I know talk about their God-fearing Yiddishe Mommes who lit candles competently at the appointed times and believed what their men taught them. I had to stop Ma lighting candles because she didn't know the difference between ritual flames and burning us all to a cinder. Later on in life, Ma began to believe. She knew why the world was so hopelessly wrong, she said. It was because the Almighty was a "he" and not a "she" and the only really responsible creatures who could run the show were all shes. Look at grandpa and grandma, she said, or her and Dad.

Before I left "the House of Life" (words written on the gates of many Jewish cemeteries), I purloined another wilting baccarat rose, because she had taught me real religion which is "generosity of spirit". I miss her, my not quite but more than Yiddishe Momme. When it's my turn to go to the House of Life, I'll try and catch her up. I want to tell her a quip I'd heard: "The place of the mother is in the wrong." She'd like that!

Rabbi Lionel Blue OBE

PRAYERS TO THE BLESSED VIRGIN MARY

We Pray With Mary

May the heart of Mary be in each Christian
to proclaim the greatness of the Lord;
May her spirit be in everyone to exult in God.

(St Ambrose)

The Magnificat

My soul glorifies the Lord,
My spirit rejoices in God, my Saviour.
He looks on his servant in her lowliness,
Henceforth all ages will call me blessed.

The Almighty works marvels for me
Holy his name!
His mercy is from age to age,
On those who fear him.
He puts forth his arm in strength
And scatters the proud-hearted.
He casts the mighty from their thrones
And raises the lowly.
He fills the starving with good things,
Sends the rich away empty.
He protects Israel, his servant,

Remembering his mercy,
The mercy promised to our fathers,
To Abraham and his sons for ever.

(Morning and Evening Prayer, Collins, 1976 ISBN 0 00 599565 05)

Hail Mary

Hail, Mary, full of grace, the Lord is with thee: blessed art thou among women, and blessed is the fruit of thy womb, Jesus. Holy Mary, Mother of God, pray for us sinners, now, and at the hour of our death. Amen.

(A Simple Prayer Book, Catholic Truth Society, 1999 ISBN 1 86082 074 3)

The Angelus

May be said morning, noon and night, to put us in mind that God the Son became man for our salvation.

V. The Angel of the Lord declared unto Mary:
R. And she conceived by the Holy Spirit. Hail Mary...
V. Behold the handmaid of the Lord:
R. Be it done unto me according to thy word. Hail Mary...
V. And the Word was Made Flesh:
R. And dwelt among us. Hail Mary...
V. Pray for us, O holy Mother of God.
R. That we may be made worthy of the promises of Christ.

Let us pray

Pour forth, we beseech you, O Lord, your grace into our hearts, that we, to whom the Incarnation of Christ, your Son, was made known by the message of an angel, may be brought by his passion and cross + to the glory of his resurrection, through the same Christ our Lord. R. Amen.

(A Simple Prayer Book, Catholic Truth Society, 1999, ISBN 1 86082 074 3)

The Regina Cæli

Replaces the Angelus during Easter-time.

O Queen of heaven, rejoice! Alleluia.
For he whom you did merit to bear, Alleluia,
Has risen as he said. Alleluia.
Pray for us to God. Alleluia.

V. Rejoice and be glad, O Virgin Mary, Alleluia.
R. For the Lord has risen indeed, Alleluia.

Let us pray

God our Father, you give joy to the world by the resurrection of your Son, our Lord Jesus Christ. Through the prayers of his mother, the Virgin Mary, bring us to the happiness of eternal life. We ask this through our Lord Jesus Christ, your Son, who lives and reigns with you and the Holy Spirit, one God, for ever and ever. R. Amen.

(A Simple Prayer Book, Catholic Truth Society, 1999, ISBN 1 86082 074 3)

The Salve Regina

Hail, holy Queen, mother of mercy; hail, our life, our sweetness, and our hope! To you do we cry; poor banished children of Eve; to you do we send up our sighs, mourning and weeping in this vale of tears. Turn then, most gracious advocate, your eyes of mercy towards us; and after this our exile, show to us the blessed fruit of your womb, Jesus. O clement, O loving, O sweet Virgin Mary.

(A Simple Prayer Book. Catholic Truth Society. 1999. ISBN 1 86082 074 3)

The Mysteries of the Rosary

The Joyful Mysteries
The Annunciation.
The Visitation.
The Nativity.
The Presentation.
The Finding in the Temple.

The Mysteries of Light
The Baptism in the Jordan.
The Wedding at Cana.
The Proclamation of the Kingdom of God.
The Transfiguration.
The Institution of the Eucharist.

The Sorrowful Mysteries
The Agony in the Garden.
The Scourging at the Pillar.
The Crowning with Thorns.
The Carrying of the Cross.
The Crucifixion.

The Glorious Mysteries
The Resurrection.
The Ascension.
The Descent of the Holy Spirit.
The Assumption.
The Crowning of Our Lady in Heaven, and the Glory of all the Saints.

(Rosarium Virginis Mariae. Catholic Truth Society. 2002. ISBN 1 86082 179 0)

V. Queen of the Most Holy Rosary,
   pray for us.
R. That we may be made worthy of the promises
   of Christ.

Let us pray
O God, whose only-begotten Son, by his life, death and resurrection has purchased for us the rewards of eternal life; grant we beseech you, that meditating upon these mysteries in the most holy rosary of the Blessed Virgin Mary, we may both imitate what they contain and obtain what they promise, through the same Christ Our Lord. Amen.

(Treasury of the Holy Spirit. Hodder & Stoughton. 1984.)

Prayer Based on the Mysteries of the Rosary

O Mary, mother of the Church,
Teach us to accept God's will, in the spirit of
the annunciation;
Visit us in our need, as you visited Elizabeth;
Bring us forth in grace, as you brought forth
Jesus in the flesh;
Present us in the temple of the Father;
And take us, after this life's journey,
To find Jesus in his Father's house.
Obtain for us the courage to be one
with Jesus in his agony,
And to say "Father, your will be done;"
Grant that "through his wounds",
we may be healed;
Teach us the meekness of our king crowned
with thorns,
And how to carry our cross daily;
That we may "Know the fellowship of his
sufferings" on Mount Calvary.
And when the hour comes to leave
this world, grant
that we may "know the power of his resurrection;"
And ascend to that home prepared for us;
O Mary, sweet spouse of the Spirit,
grant that we may share in the out-pouring of the
Holy Ghost;
And after this our exile, rejoice in the glory of
your assumption.
And coronation in heaven. Amen.

(*Good News of the Rosary, Gabriel M Harty, OP 1967.*)

The Litany of Loreto

Lord have mercy.
Lord have mercy.
Christ have mercy.
Christ have mercy.
Lord have mercy.
Lord have mercy.
Christ hear us.
Christ graciously hear us.

God the Father of heaven,
have mercy on us.
God the Son, Redeemer of the world,
have mercy on us.
God the Holy Spirit,
have mercy on us.
Holy Trinity, one God,
have mercy on us.

Holy Mary,
pray for us.
Holy Mother of God,
pray for us.
Holy Virgin of virgins,
pray for us.

Mother of Christ,
pray for us.
Mother of the Church,
pray for us.
Mother of divine grace,
pray for us.
Mother most pure,
pray for us.
Mother most chaste,
pray for us.
Mother inviolate,
pray for us.
Mother undefiled,
pray for us.
Mother most lovable,
pray for us.
Mother most admirable,
pray for us.
Mother of good counsel,
pray for us.
Mother of our Creator,
pray for us.
Mother of our Saviour,
pray for us.

Virgin most prudent,
pray for us.
Virgin most venerable,
pray for us.

Virgin most renowned,
pray for us.
Virgin most powerful,
pray for us.
Virgin most merciful,
pray for us.
Virgin most faithful,
pray for us.

Mirror of Justice,
pray for us.
Seat of wisdom,
pray for us.
Cause of our joy,
pray for us.
Spiritual vessel,
pray for us.
Vessel of honour,
pray for us.
Singular vessel of devotion,
pray for us.
Mystical rose,
pray for us.
Tower of David,
pray for us.
Tower of ivory,
pray for us.
House of gold,
pray for us.

Ark of the covenant,
pray for us.
Gate of heaven,
pray for us.
Morning Star,
pray for us.
Health of the sick,
pray for us.
Refuge of sinners,
pray for us.
Comfort of the afflicted,
pray for us.
Help of Christians,
pray for us.

Queen of Angels,
pray for us.
Queen of Patriarchs,
pray for us.
Queen of Prophets,
pray for us.
Mother of Apostles,
pray for us.
Queen of Martyrs,
pray for us.
Queen of Confessors,
pray for us.
Queen of Virgins,
pray for us.

Queen of all Saints,
pray for us.
Queen conceived without original sin,
pray for us.
Queen assumed into heaven,
pray for us.
Queen of the most holy Rosary,
pray for us.
Queen of Peace,
pray for us.
Queen of the Family,
pray for us.

Lamb of God, you take away the sins of the world,
spare us, O Lord.
Lamb of God, you take away the sins of the world,
graciously hear us, O Lord.
Lamb of God, you take away the sins of the world,
have mercy on us.
V. Pray for us, O holy Mother of God.
R. That we may be made worthy of the promises
of Christ.

Let us pray
Lord God, give to your people the joy of
continual health in mind and body. With the
prayers of the Virgin Mary to help us, guide us
through the sorrows of this life to eternal
happiness in the life to come. Grant this through
our Lord Jesus Christ, your Son, who lives and

reigns with you and the Holy Spirit, one God, for ever and ever. R. Amen.

(A Simple Prayer Book. Catholic Truth Society. 1999. ISBN 1 86082 974 3)

The Seven Sorrows

The Prophecy of Simeon.
The Flight into Egypt.
The Loss of the Child Jesus in the Temple.
Mary Meets Jesus on the Way to Calvary.
Jesus Dies on the Cross.
Mary Receives the Body of Jesus in Her Arms.
The Body of Jesus is Placed in the Tomb.

In Honour of the Seven Sorrows of Our Lady

I grieve for thee, sorrowing Mary, in the affliction of thy tender heart at hearing the prophecy of the aged and holy Simeon. Dear Mother, by thy heart thus afflicted, obtain for me the virtue of humility and the gift of the holy fear of God. Hail Mary...

I grieve for thee, sorrowing Mary, in the anxiety of thy affectionate heart during the flight into Egypt and thy sojourn there. Dear Mother, by thy heart thus racked, obtain for me the virtue of generosity, especially towards the poor, and the gift of piety. Hail Mary...

I grieve for thee, sorrowing Mary, in the anguish that beset thy troubled heart at the loss of thy beloved Jesus. Dear Mother, by thy heart thus riven, obtain for me the virtue of chastity and the gift of knowledge. Hail, Mary...

I grieve for thee, sorrowing Mary, in thy heartfelt dismay at meeting Jesus as he carried his cross. Dear Mother, by thy heart thus dismayed, obtain for me the virtue of patience and the gift of fortitude. Hail, Mary...

I grieve for thee, sorrowing Mary, in the martyrdom thy generous heart endured in standing by Jesus in his agony. Dear Mother, by thy heart thus tortured, obtain for me the virtue of self-control and the gift of prudence.
Hail, Mary...

I grieve for thee, sorrowing Mary, in the wounding of thy compassionate heart when the side of Jesus was stabbed with a lance and his beloved heart was pierced. Dear Mother, by thy heart thus transfixed, obtain for me the virtue of brotherly love and the gift of understanding.
Hail, Mary...

I grieve for thee, sorrowing Mary, in the pangs thy loving heart felt at the burial of Jesus. Dear Mother, by thy heart thus wrung, obtain for me the virtue of perseverance and the gift of wisdom.
Hail, Mary...

V. Pray for us, Virgin most sorrowful.
R. That we may become worthy of the promises of Christ.

Let us pray

May we be aided at thy mercy-seat, Lord Jesus Christ, now and at the hour of our death, by the pleading of the blessed Virgin Mary, thy Mother, whose most holy soul was pierced, in the hour of thy sufferings by a sword of sorrow: through thee, Jesus Christ, Saviour of the world, who livest and reignest with the Father and the Holy Spirit for ever and ever.

(The Manual of Catholic Prayer, Burns & Oates, 1962.)

The Memorare

Remember, O most loving Virgin Mary, that it is a thing unheard of, that anyone ever had recourse to your protection, implored your help, or sought your intercession, and was left forsaken. Filled therefore with confidence in your goodness I fly to you, O Mother, Virgin of virgins. To you I come, before you I stand, a sorrowful sinner. Despise not my poor words, O Mother of the Word of God, but graciously hear and grant my prayer.

(A Simple Prayer Book, Catholic Truth Society, 1999. ISBN 1 86082 074 3)

Alma Redemptoris Mater

Loving Mother of the Redeemer, gate of heaven, star of the sea, assist your people who have fallen yet strive to rise again. To the wonderment of nature you bore your Creator, yet remained a virgin after as before. You who received Gabriel's joyful greeting, have pity on us poor sinners.

(The Manual of Prayers, Pontifical North American College, Rome, 1998. ISBN 1 890177 03 2)

Ave Regina Cælorum

Hail, O Queen of Heaven Enthroned!
Hail, by angels mistress owned!
Root of Jesse, Gate of morn,
Whence the world's true light was born.
Glorious Virgin, joy to you!
Loveliest whom in Heaven we see.
Fairest thou where all are fair,
Plead with Christ our sins to spare.

(The Manual of Prayers, Pontifical North American College, Rome, 1998. ISBN : 890177 03 2)

Sub Tuum Præsidium

We fly to thy protection, O holy Mother of God, despise not our petitions in our necessities, but deliver us always from all dangers, O glorious and blessed Virgin.

(The Manual of Prayers, Pontifical North American College, Rome, 1998. ISBN 1 890177 03 2)

From the Liturgy of St John Chrysostom

It is truly right that we bless you, O Theotokos, God-bearer, the ever blessed and most pure Mother of our God: more honoured than the Cherubim, and more glorious beyond compare than the Seraphim, for you, undefiled, gave birth to God the Word: therefore we praise you, O true Mother of God.

(A Book of Hours and Other Catholic Devotion. Canterbury Press. 1998. ISBN 1 85311 191 0)

Prayer of Saint Ephraem the Syrian

Blessed Virgin, immaculate and pure, you are the sinless Mother of your Son, who is the mighty Lord of the universe. Since you are holy and inviolate, the hope of the hopeless and sinful, I sing your praises. I praise you as full of every grace, for you bore the God-Man. I venerate you; I invoke you and implore your aid. Holy and Immaculate Virgin, help me in every need that presses upon me and free me from all the temptations of the devil. Be my intercessor and advocate at the hour of death and judgement. Deliver me from the fire that is not extinguished and from the outer darkness. Make me worthy of the glory of your Son, O dearest and most kind Virgin Mother. You indeed are my most secure

and only hope, for you are holy in the sight of God, to whom be honour and glory, majesty and power forever. Amen.

(The Manual of Prayers. Pontifical North American College. Rome. 1998. ISBN 1 890177 03 2)

To the Immaculate Virgin

Hail, thee, O most Blessed Virgin, Cause of our Joy! Through you has been repaired the curse of our first mother: through you we have received once more blessings of grace, adoption as children of God! Hail, O Virgin Mary – name most sweet! Hail, O Mother of God, most holy and most blessed! By the ineffable grace with which the Holy Spirit adored you as His Spouse and as the Mother of the Son of God, we beg of you to obtain from God the Son, that we, by the sanctification of that same Holy Spirit, become worthy Temples of His Glory. Amen.

(Saint Andrew of Crete) (The Manual of Prayers. Pontifical North American College. Rome. 1998. ISBN 1 890177 03 2)

Prayer of St John Damascene

The Angelic host, the race of men, all creation rejoices over thee, Mary, for thou art full of grace, a hallowed temple, a spiritual paradise. From thee, most glorious of virgins, our God took flesh; he who at the beginning of time was already God became thy child. He made thy womb his throne;

he, whom the heavens cannot hold, found there his resting-place. All creation rejoices over thee. Glory be thine, Mary, for thou art full of grace.

(The Manual of Catholic Prayer. Burns & Oates, 1962.)

You Are Fair, O Mary

You are fair, O Mary: the original stain is not in you. You are the glory of Jerusalem. You are the joy of Israel. You are the great honour of our people. You are the advocate of sinners. O Mary, O Mary, Virgin most prudent, Mother most merciful, pray for us. Intercede for us with our Lord Jesus Christ. Amen.

(The Manual of Prayers. Pontifical North American College. Rome. 1998. ISBN 1 890177 03 2)

Maria, Mater Gratiæ

Mary, Mother of grace, Mother of mercy, protect me from the enemy and receive me at the hour of death.

(The Manual of Prayers. Pontifical North American College. Rome. 1998. ISBN 1 890177 03 2)

Sancta Maria, Succurre Miseris

Holy Mary, hasten to the aid of the afflicted, support the fainthearted. Comfort the sorrowful, pray for your people, intercede on behalf of the clergy, intercede for devout women; may all who

celebrate your holy memory come to know your assistance.

(The Manual of Prayers. Pontifical North American College. Rome. 1998. ISBN 1 890177 03 2)

Prayer of St Ildephonsus

I beg you, holy Virgin that I may have Jesus from the Holy Spirit, by whom you brought Jesus forth. May my soul receive Jesus through the Holy Spirit by whom your flesh conceived Jesus. May I love Jesus in the Holy Spirit in whom you adore Jesus as Lord and gaze upon him as your Son.

(To Honour Mary. Catholic Truth Society, 1974)

Prayer of Erasmus to Our Lady of Walsingham

O alone of all women, Mother and Virgin, Mother most happy, Virgin most pure, now we, impure as we are, come to see thee who art all pure; we salute thee: we worship thee as how we may with our humble offerings: may thy Son grant us, that imitating thy most holy manners, we also, by the grace of the Holy Ghost, may deserve spiritually to conceive the Lord Jesus in our inmost soul, and once conceived, never to lose him. Amen

(Pilgrim's Manual. Anglican Shrine of Our Lady of Walsingham, 1976)

Prayer of St Aloysius

To Thee, O holy Mary, my sovereign Mistress, to thy blessed trust and special charge, and to the bosom of thy mercy, this day and every day, and at the hour of my death I commend myself, my soul and my body: to thee I commit all my hope and all my consolation, my distresses and my miseries, my life and the end thereof; that through thy most holy intercession, and through thy merits, all my works may be directed and disposed, according to thy will and the will of thy Son. Amen.

(A Book of Hours and Other Catholic Devotions. Canterbury Press. 1998. ISBN 1 85311 191 0)

Prayer of Our Lady of Lourdes

Ever immaculate Virgin, Mother of mercy, health of the sick, refuge of sinners, comfort of the afflicted, you know my needs, my troubles, my sufferings; cast on me a look of pity. By appearing in the grotto of Lourdes, you were pleased to make it a privileged sanctuary, from which you dispense your favours, and already many sufferers have obtained the cure of their infirmities, both spiritual and physical. I come, therefore, with the most unbounded confidence to implore your maternal intercession. Obtain, most loving mother, my requests, through Jesus Christ your Son our Lord. Amen.

(Treasury of the Holy Spirit. Hodder & Stoughton. 1984.)

Prayer of Abbé Perreyve to Our Lady of Lourdes

Holy Virgin, amid thy glory do not forget the sorrows of earth. Cast a look of pity on those who are in pain, on those who are struggling against difficulties, and daily tasting of life's bitter cup. Take pity on those who have loved one another and now are parted, on lonely hearts, on wavering faith, on those we tenderly love. Take pity on those who weep and pray, take pity on those who are afraid. Grant hope and peace to all.

(The Manual of Catholic Prayer. Burns & Oates. 1962.)

Prayer to Mary our Mother

O Blessed Virgin Mary, unspotted Mother of my God and Saviour Jesus Christ, be a mother to me, since your adorable Son has been pleased to call us all his brethren, and to recommend us all to thee in the person of his beloved disciple. Take me and mine under your holy protection, and continually represent to the eternal Father, on our behalf, the merits of the death and passion of your Son, our Saviour.

(A Book of Hours and Other Catholic Devotions. Canterbury Press. 1998. ISBN 1 85311 191 0)

Prayer for the Church and for Unity

O Mary, Mother of Jesus, the glory of body and soul you now possess in heaven shows us the happiness that we will enjoy when the Church reaches her perfect state in the world to come. As long as life remains in this world, you shine forth from heaven, as the sign of sure hope and comfort for the people of God on their pilgrimage.

We are glad to be united with all Christians who give fitting honour to you, as the mother of Our Lord and Saviour, and especially with the Eastern Christians, who have always honoured you with such great love and devotion.

With all believers in Christ, we pour out urgent and constant prayers to you for the whole Church. As you gave support with your prayers, when the Church began its life of service on earth, and as you are now raised above all your fellow members of the church glorious in heaven, pray to your Son for us as we live and work in that same Church today. Continue to pray for us, until all people in the world, Christians and those who do not yet know Christ, are happily gathered in peace and unity, into the one people of God, for the glory of the most holy and undivided Trinity. Amen.

(Marian Devotions for Today; Goodliffe Neal. 1971. Leaflet.)

Prayer to Our Lady of the Harvest

O Mary, you are the 'good ground' on which the seed fell. You have brought forth fruit a hundredfold. Draw us close to your loving heart and keep us there in gentle lowliness and perfect trust. Teach us to receive the Spirit as you did to open our hearts to the Sacred Word, to ponder it in silence and yield a rich harvest. Teach us to be apostles of love.

(Ruth Etchaways) (A Book of Hours and Other Catholic Devotions. Canterbury Press. 1998. ISBN 1 85311 191 0)

Act of Consecration to the Blessed Virgin

I venerate you with all my heart, O Virgin most holy, above all angels and saints in paradise, as the daughter of the Eternal Father, and to you I consecrate my soul with all its powers.

Hail Mary....

I venerate you with all my heart, O Virgin most holy, above all angels and saints in paradise, as the Mother of the only begotten Son, and to you I consecrate my body with all its senses.

Hail Mary....

I venerate you with all my heart, O Virgin most holy, above all angels and saints in paradise, as the beloved Spouse of the Spirit of God, and to you I consecrate my heart and all its affections, imploring you to obtain from the most Holy Trinity, all means of salvation. Hail Mary…

(The Manual of Prayers. Pontifical North American College. Rome. 1998. ISBN 1 890177 03 2)

Totus Tuus

Totus tuus ego sum, et omnia mea tua sunt,
O Virgo, super omnia benedicta.
I am all yours, and all that is mine is yours,
O Virgin, blessed above all.

(Saint Louis-Marie Grignon de Montfort)

(The Manual of Prayers. Pontifical North American College. Rome. 1998. ISBN 1 890177 03 2)

Mother of the Living

O Mary,
bright dawn of the new world,
Mother of the living,
to you do we entrust the cause of life:
Look down, O Mother,
upon the vast numbers
of babies not allowed to be born,
of the poor whose lives are made difficult,
of men and women
who are victims of brutal violence,
of the elderly and the sick killed
by indifference or out of misguided mercy.

Grant that all who believe in your Son
may proclaim the Gospel of life
with honesty and love to the people of our time.
Obtain for them the grace
to accept that Gospel
as a gift ever new,
the joy of celebrating it with gratitude
throughout their lives and the courage to bear
witness to it
resolutely, in order to build,
together with all people of good will,
the civilization of truth and love,
to the praise and glory of God,
the Creator and lover of life.

(Pope John Paul II)

(Evangelium Vitae. Catholic Truth Society. 1995. ISBN 0 85183 951 7)

O Jesus, Living in Mary

O Jesus, living in Mary, come and live in your servants, in the spirit of holiness, in the fullness of your power, in the perfection of your ways, in the truth of your virtues, in the communion of your mysteries. Rule over every adverse power, in your Spirit, for the glory of the Father. Amen.

(Jean Jacques Olier, S.S.) (The Manual of Prayers. Pontifical North American College. Rome. 1998. ISBN 1 890177 03 2)